STRIDERS

T0315959

Amazing Caves

Contents

Published in the UK by
Scholastic Education, 2024
Scholastic Distribution Centre, Bosworth Avenue,
Tournament Fields, Warwick, CV34 6UQ
Scholastic Ireland, 89E Lagan Road, Dublin
Industrial Estate, Glasnevin, Dublin, D11 HP5F

SCHOLASTIC and associated logos are
trademarks and/or registered trademarks of
Scholastic Inc.
www.scholastic.co.uk

© 2024 Scholastic

1 2 3 4 5 6 7 8 9   4 5 6 7 8 9 0 1 2 3

Printed by Ashford Colour Press

This book is made of materials from
well-managed, FSC®-certified forests
and other controlled sources.

MIX
Paper from
responsible sources
FSC
www.fsc.org   FSC® C011748

A CIP catalogue record for this book is available
from the British Library.

ISBN 978-0702-32729-2

Every effort has been made to trace copyright
holders for the works reproduced in this
publication, and the publishers apologise for any
inadvertent omissions.

Author
Rachel Russ

Editorial team
Rachel Morgan, Vicki Yates, Sasha Morton,
Alison Gilbert

Design team
Dipa Mistry, Andrea Lewis and We Are Grace

Photographs
Cover Zarela Simon/Shutterstock
p4–5 cb_travel/Shutterstock
p8 Sascha Burkard/Shutterstock
p1, 4, 8, 10, 14, 17, 18, 24 (background)
Isared Honghin/Shutterstock
p6–7 (background) Hamid Ishaq 12/Shutterstock
p9 Kim Willems/Shutterstock
p10, 17 (map) Cvijovic Zarko/Shutterstock
p10–11 ThamKC/Shutterstock
p11 (plane) Kalinsky/Shutterstock
p12–13 Breck P. Kent/Shutterstock
p14–15 tornado98/iStock
p14 (snake) Thai Tea/Shutterstock
p14 (gecko) Pavaphon Supanantananont/
Shutterstock
p16 Scott Biales DitchTheMap/Shutterstock
p16 (bats insert) Agami Photo Agency/
Shutterstock
p17 Charlene Manet/Shutterstock
p18–19 Marques/Shutterstock
p20–21 Josemar Franco/Shutterstock
p22–23 Tatiana Kovaleva/Shutterstock

Illustrations
p6–7 QBS Learning

How to use this book

This book practises these letters and letter sounds:

o (as in 'over')	i (as in 'kind')	a (as in 'gazing')
a-e (as in 'waves')	i-e (as in 'time')	o-e (as in 'home')
e-e (as in 'these')		

Here are some of the words in the book that use the sounds above:

caves   over   inside   wildlife   created

This book uses these common tricky words:

**are   they   of   when   into   water   pushes
the   could   to   some   their   were   by
was   people**

Before reading

- Read the title and look at the cover. Discuss what the book might be about.

During reading

- If necessary, sound it out and then blend the sounds to read the word: c-r-a-ck, crack.
- Pause every so often to talk about the information.

After reading

- Talk about what has been read.
- Use the index on page 24 to select any pages to revisit.

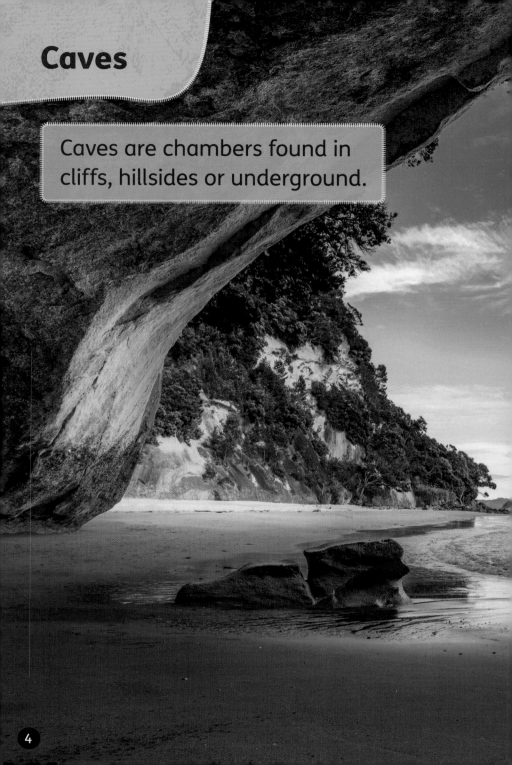

Caves

Caves are chambers found in cliffs, hillsides or underground.

They form over hundreds of thousands of years.

How Caves Form

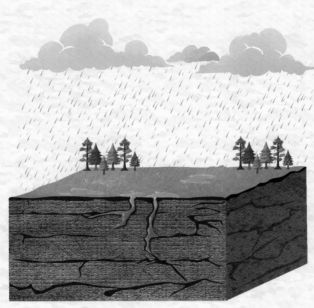

1

On land, most caves are formed when rain drips into limestone (a kind of rock).

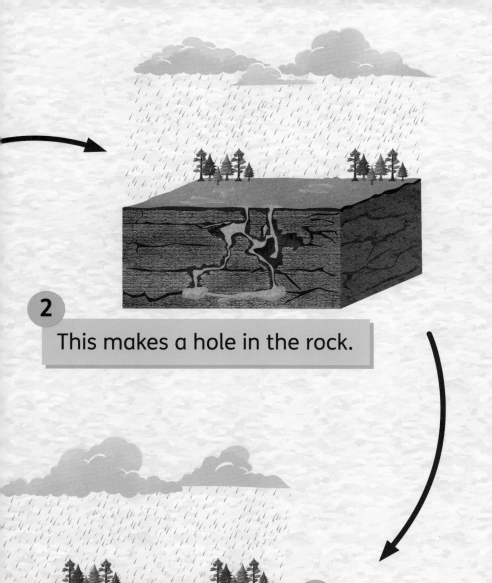

2 This makes a hole in the rock.

3 It gets bigger over time.

Sea caves appear on coastlines when waves keep crashing into cliffs.

Water pushes into a crack until it opens up. Over time a cave is created.

Amazing Caves

The biggest cave chamber on the planet is in Borneo.

Borneo

Lots of jumbo jets could fit inside it.

Stalactites form as water drips from a cave roof.

stalactite

Stalagmites can form at the bottom as water drips down.

stalagmite

Cave Wildlife

Caves are home to wildlife such as fish, spiders and reptiles.

snake

gecko

Some adapt to complete darkness.

As it has no need to see, this salamander is blind.

Bats go outside in the evening to find food. They return to their cave at dawn.

These lights might look like shimmering jewels, but they are insects.

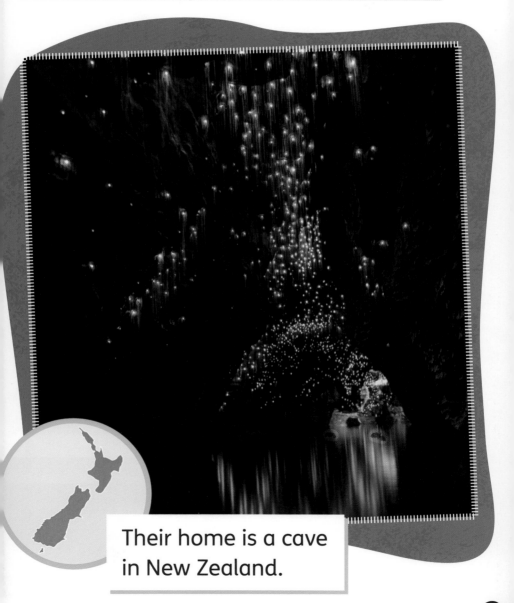

Their home is a cave in New Zealand.

Humans and Caves

Amazing man-made cave homes can be found across the globe.

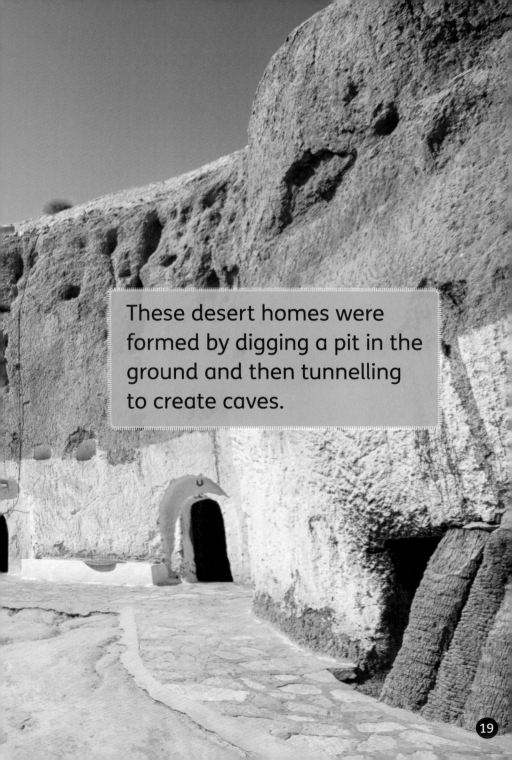

These desert homes were formed by digging a pit in the ground and then tunnelling to create caves.

This cave painting was created by humans tens of thousands of years ago.

Experts assume the people in it are star gazing.

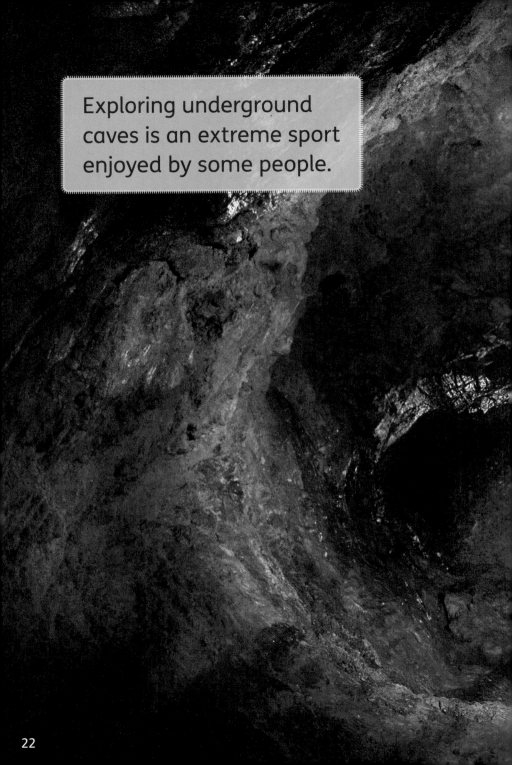

Exploring underground caves is an extreme sport enjoyed by some people.

Index